The right of Judy Rose to be identified as the author of this
work has been asserted in accordance with Section 78
of the Copyright, Designs and Patents Act 1988

The book cover is copyright to Judy Rose

This book is published by
Grosvenor House Publishing Ltd
Link House
140 The Broadway, Tolworth, Surrey, KT6 7HT.
www.grosvenorhousepublishing.co.uk

This book is sold subject to the conditions that it shall not, by way of
trade or otherwise, be lent, resold, hired out or otherwise circulated
without the author's or publisher's prior consent in any form of
binding or cover other than that in which it is published and
without a similar condition including this condition being
imposed on the subsequent purchaser.

This book is a work of fiction. Any resemblance to
people or events, past or present, is purely coincidental.

A CIP record for this book
is available from the British Library

ISBN 978-1-80381-632-6

It really is a tad unfair,
And quite hard to ignore;
That 'morning after' feeling
When there wasn't 'a night before.'

I rush upstairs with purpose,
Hurl open bedroom door.
Now just need to remember
What the hell I came up for?

To minimise the wrinkles
And flaws in my complexion
I just remove my glasses
When I look at my reflection.

Never too late to learn fresh skills
And such exciting news;
I have become quite brilliant at
'The Art of the Afternoon Snooze.'

Laughter's the best medicine.
Yes, very true and wise,
Plus thirty facial muscles used;
My kind of exercise.

I weigh myself
And get a shock...
Then common sense prevails.
There's really no cause for alarm;
It's just my faulty scales.

Some parts of me look extra tired
And I regret to say
I rarely stick my neck out;
It gives the game away.
And so I opt for polo necks,
A scarf can help as well.
When warmer weather comes
it's tough
And on the beach
It's hell!

Nothing else can make my day
And cause such joy and mirth
As scrolling down
And down
And down
To find my year of birth.

There's a question
I ask endlessly
Though the answer's crystal clear,
It's my 'Menopausal Mantra'
Is it me
Or is it hot in here?

When life just gets annoying
And I need a little break
I take deep breaths
And think this thought;
Thank goodness there is
CAKE!

I try hard not to look my age
But now admit defeat;
A very elderly gentleman
Just offered me his seat!

Just watched a film.
What was it called?
It's great. A real 'must see'.
It stars the chap from thingy,
You know...name starts with P.
Or maybe B. Whatever.
He married what's-her-name?
The one who used to be in *Friends*.
They split up. Such a shame.
So please do try and see it,
You really won't regret it.
Just like the one about the sharks...
Once seen you won't forget it!

For age defying strategies
I have some cunning plans;
To pass as ten years younger
I just sit on my hands.

Be careful what you wish for,
Sometimes you just can't win.
I wished
That I had lots more hair
And I got it
On my chin.

Embrace each year that passes
And do remember please
That age is just
'All in the mind'
(Not to mention hips, back, knees.)

We older models know what's what.
We're sassy, savvy, brave.
We've earned the right
To speak our minds
And also
Misbehave!

My purse found in the bread bin!
Though pleased it must be said
It rather begs the question
Where on earth I put the bread?

High time to reinvent yourself
Reveal those skills, that flair.
Yes, now's the time to show the world
Your genius laid bare.

I sense that things
Are moving south.
Not what I want to see.
You've got a lot to answer for
YOU BASTARD
GRAVITY!

I have a special mantra
And philosophy I follow.
Each day I sit
And chant these words;
'The Diet starts tomorrow.'

In future
Concentrating
In the bathroom
Might be wise;
Just patted
Athlete's foot cream
Very gently
Round both eyes.

I may seem pretty harmless
But I say advisedly
I'm a menopausal woman
SO DO NOT MESS WITH ME!

Passing by my mirror
I catch sight of my reflection.
It's not an image that inspires
A more in-depth inspection.
But I am not alarmed at all
By the vision that appears;
That mirror distorts everything...
It's been like that for years.

I'm laden down with shopping,
And tired
But worse by far
I simply can't remember
Where I parked
THE BLOODY CAR!

Who would have guessed the changes
That later life would bring.
Four words I never dreamt I'd say;
I JUST LOVE
GARDENING.

The woman of 'a certain age'
Will never leap about.
Skipping is a no no
And star-jumping is out.
But daily life has perils too;
She knows, accepts, regrets
That coughing, laughing, sneezing
May have knock-on effects.

The ticket sales girl got my goat.
No questions.
No debate.
Just took one look
And gave me
The Senior Citizens rate.

Bikini-clad upon the beach
Observe with some distress,
Pre-holiday crash-diet
Was not complete success!

So much research on alcohol
You don't know where to start.
But really love the one that says
Red wine's good for your heart.

I really wish my body
Had a button I could press
To carry out a simple task,
That function called
REFRESH.

Not sure how I can put this right?
Quite frankly it's a bummer.
Have just sent spouse's
'Love You 💜' text
To my very fit young plumber!

I'm really struggling with the zip,
I'm going to split the seams.
It must be my damn washing machine
That's gone and shrunk my jeans.

Among the revelations
That getting older brings
Is 'having a hot body'
Can mean two different things!

I've been on hold for ages now.
I'm climbing up the wall.
Plus now cannot remember
Why the hell
I made the call.

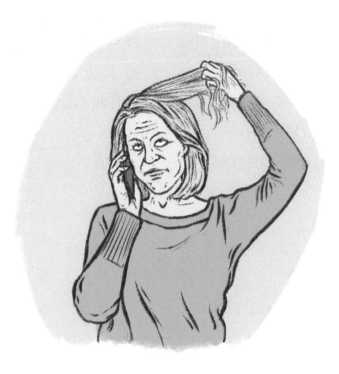

I'd really like to exercise.
But don't; you never know
The consequences and the risks;
Which bit of me might 'go'.
And there's another reason...
A good one;
Strictly speaking
I'm trying hard to minimise
The sound
Of chronic creaking.

Fine weather.
Shorts are just the thing
But wish that someone please
Would come out with
A magic cream
To tackle
Wrinkly knees.

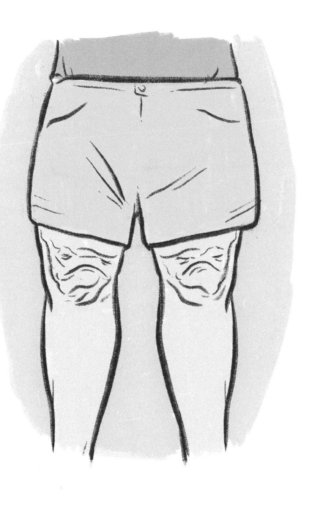

Across the street
I spot a friend.
Rush up, arms open wide.
Now close
I see a stranger
Looking pretty terrified.

How to shed that baby weight?
A mystery to me.
And quite a lengthy one at that;
That baby's
Thirty-three.

Remember with each passing year
As you turn another page
The more important it becomes
To never act your age.

To check on 'pertness of the breast'
I did the Pencil Test.
I failed of course,
It was a flop.
I felt most unimpressed.
But things got worse;
At bedtime
I found to my dismay
The wretched little pencil
Had been nestling there
All day!

I steer clear of self check-outs
As there is nothing scarier
Than my unexpected tantrum
In the blasted bagging area.

Magnifying mirrors
Should come with a Health Warning.
DANGER
NEVER USE THIS.
FIRST THING IN THE MORNING.

I've loads of clothes
From way back when
That fit and I still wear.
The fact they're mainly
Hats, gloves, scarves
Is neither here nor there.

I juggled, multi-tasked through life
As worker, wife and mother,
But now can't even talk and do;
It's one thing
Or the other.

I keep the biscuits out of reach.
High up.
Extremely wise.
Each time I stretch
To reach the tin
It counts as exercise.

The air is turning very blue.
I howl with sheer frustration.
I've muddled up my password
With my user information.
Alas this trip to cyber-space
Will have to wait till later;
I can't remember where I hid
My oh-so-secret data!

I gave up meat
One week ago.
I knew it would be hell.
But apart from a burger
And my Sunday roast,
Things are going pretty well.

With age I sadly must concede
My make-up needs will change
Next stop
The DIY store
For Polyfilla's Skincare Range.

I know I bought
Some Christmas gifts
A while back,
As you do,
But what
Or where I put them
I do not have a clue.

Some Christmas treats are healthy
And mince pies lead the way;
The raisins, currants, apples
Are three of my five-a day.

My New Year's Resolution
Is guaranteed win-win.
It's easy and achievable;
I'm going to drink
More gin.

The periods, the PMT,
The Menopause.
All tough.
Plus plenty more that's on the list
Of 'tricky female stuff'.
But do not be despondent
Just remember if you can...
Things could have been
A great deal worse;
You could have been
A man!

Judy Rose started writing poetry many decades ago when she realised she needed an outlet to express her experiences of the ups and downs of motherhood, unsuccessful attempts at being a domestic goddess and the fruitless pursuit of acquiring the body of Elle Macpherson. Sadly there have been few improvements over the years and now, with the passing of time, she has turned her attention to the many challenges of middle age and beyond.

Also by Judy Rose
On The Plus Side
(A little book of Positivity and
Optimism for Vintage Models)

Follow Judy on https://www.facebook.com/womans.world.observed.

Daniel Weisz studied illustration at the University of Westminster and now lives in Seaford with his lovely wife Cara, their two young sons Lenny and Ned and their Cavapoo Peggy-Sue. He produces artwork for a wide variety of clients as well as his own range of cards, prints and gifts.

Milton Keynes UK
Ingram Content Group UK Ltd.
UKHW051006231123
432971UK00011B/100